HOW TO FIND INFORMATION

•

HEALTH CARE

By BRUCE MADGE

THE BRITISH LIBRARY

How to find information: health care
ISBN 0-7123-0873-3

Published by:
The British Library
96 Euston Road
London NW1 2DB

British Library Cataloguing-in-Publication Data
A catalogue record is available for this book from the British Library

Desktop publishing by Concerto, Leighton Buzzard, Bedfordshire
Tel: 01525 378757

Printed in Great Britain by Atheneum Press Ltd, Gateshead, Tyne and Wear

Contents

Introduction

Health is important to everyone and provides employment to a huge number of health care professionals. It appears regularly in the news and there is a great demand from both patients and the professional to find the correct information about various treatments and 'health scares'.

In the United Kingdom alone, the National Health Service is the country's largest employer. At some point during their training and work, all health care professionals need access to information which can be found in a library. With the increased emphasis on 'evidence-based health care' a library has become an important source of evidence for treatment and librarians are increasingly learning how critically to appraise the literature that they retrieve.

The Government sees the importance of health information to patients and it has been a constant theme in white papers since the early nineties. The recent launch of NHS Direct and NHS Direct Online underline the emphasis on the 'informed patient' and the fact that patients who know more about their particular condition often recover more quickly. However, some of these services can only provide background information. This booklet is designed to help the patient and the health professional find more 'in-depth' information on the subject of health.

Bruce Madge
December 2000

Chapter 1. Reference Sources

A library, typically, may contain the following material:

- Primary literature – i.e books, journals and theses

- Secondary literature – i.e abstracting journals and databases containing details of articles published in the 'primary' literature such as journals.

- Grey literature – that material which does not have an International Standard Book or Serial number (*see* below) i.e technical reports, reports from health authorities.

Health libraries can contain a wealth of information around the field of health care practice and usually collect in the adjacent fields of social practice and in some cases will collect in more specialised areas depending on any hospital specialities (i.e the Institute of Neurology at the National Hospital for Neurology and Neurosurgery will collect mainly in the area of diseases of the nervous system).

Many will contain a collection of key reference texts such as dictionaries and encyclopaedias. Health libraries will also have access to bibliographic databases such as Medline on either CD-ROM or on the Internet and some are beginning to offer access to electronic versions of journals as full text on the Internet.

Increasingly public libraries are becoming interested in providing health information especially to patients and this will become increasingly important as a way of getting health information to patients and the public.

Directories and other reference works

There are a large number of directories that are relevant to the health arena, those listed below are the major works to be used when looking for details of people or companies.

Dictionaries

There are three main medical dictionaries that you should find in the medical library.

- Macpherson G: *Black's Medical Dictionary.* A & C Black, London, 39th ed, 1999 is the 'English' dictionary. It is comprehensive and includes brief biographical notes, eponyms and abbreviations.

- Dorland W.A.N.: *Dorland's Illustrated Medical Dictionary*, WB Saunders, 29th ed, 2000. Comprehensive and up to date but with American spellings. A pocket version is available also.

- Stedman T.L. et al.: *Stedman's Medical Dictionary*, Lippincott, Williams and Wilkins, Philadelphia & London 27th ed, 2000. A comprehensive standard dictionary. Includes brief biographies and is also available on CD-ROM for integration into word processing packages.

For syndromes and epynomic diseases, the following two books are by far the best and most comprehensive:

- Jablonski S.: *Jablonski's Dictionary of Syndromes and Eponymic Diseases*. Krieger, Malabar, Fla. 2nd ed, 1991.

- Magalini S.I.: *Dictionary of Medical Syndromes*. Lippincott-Raven, Philadelphia, 4th ed, c. 1997

For medical quotations, there is one major source:

- Strauss M.B.: *Familiar Medical Quotations*. Little Brown, Boston. 1968. Quotations are arranged by subject and dates of birth and death are included, however, few original sources are given.

Directories

Directories are amazingly useful sources of address and basic information about a wide range of topics. There are literally hundreds of directories, so I have given the most useful ones here:

- The *Medical Directory* produced annually by FT Healthcare is the unofficial list of doctors and is compiled from questionnaires. It contains details of over 132,000 practitioners and also lists of NHS Trusts and independent hospitals. There is also now a CD-ROM version which contains more information and allows material to be downloaded.

- The *Medical Register* is the official list of registered doctors in the UK and now comes in 3 volumes and is produced annually. Most health libraries will have a copy.

- *Binleys* produce a series of very useful directories covering lists of trusts and managers as well as Primary Care Groups. Most NHS Libraries will have either the IHSM publication (*see* below) or the Binleys publications. Either can be used to get more details about addresses and NHS and private establishments.

- The *IHSM Hospital and Health Services Yearbook* annually published, also by FT Healthcare, contains a wealth of information on NHS Trusts and independent hospitals, suppliers and a comprehensive bibliography of useful publications. It is also now available as a CD-ROM which can be used to create mailing label lists.

- The *NHS Handbook* is also useful as it provides a comprehensive description of health service structure as well as the latest policy developments and up to date facts and figures. It also includes a comprehensive listing of NHS Trusts and health authorities and useful chapters about developments in the NHS. It is published annually by the NHS Confederation.

- The *World of Learning* is produced annually by Europa Publications in London and is a listing of educational, scientific and cultural establishments around the world. It includes universities and colleges, academies, research institutes, libraries and museums all arranged alphabetically by country with an index of institutions. Useful for finding out about staff details.

- The *Commonwealth Universities Yearbook* is similar to the *World of Learning* and includes data on the universities of the Commonwealth. It gives you names and addresses of staff and admission requirements and affiliations. It is produced annually by the Association of Commonwealth Universities in London.

- *A Guide to Postgraduate Degrees, Diplomas and Courses in Medicine Diplomas and Courses in Medicine* (and there is also one for dentistry) is complied annually by the Council for Postgraduate Medical Education in England and Wales on behalf of the three Councils of the United Kingdom. It has been available since 1983.

When looking for sources of funding there are two major directories which are updated annually and which are fairly comprehensive. They are:

- Charities Aid Foundation: *The Directory of Grant Making Trusts*. CAF Publication, Tonbridge, Kent is published annually as is *The Grants Register* Macmillan, London & Basingstoke.

- In the United States there is the *Directory of Biomedical and Health Care Grants* published by Oryx Press, Phoenix, Arizona.

When it comes to details of private healthcare and independent hospitals then one of the most useful directories that is published annually is:

- *Laing's Review of Private Healthcare*. Laing and Buisson, London. Is published annually and includes short articles about items of interest in private medicine as well as a comprehensive listing of all private health establishments and their staff.

Associations and professional bodies

CBD, which are based in Beckenham, Kent, produce a number of really useful directories that list organisations and associations. The two of most use are:

- *Directory of British Associations & Associations in Ireland* and

- the *Directory of European Medical Organisations*.

Both are updated regularly and list most of the associations with name, address, telephone and fax number and organisation details.

Conferences

To find details of conferences, the best tool is the *Index to Conference Proceedings* which was produced by the British Library up till 1988 when Bowker-Saur took over production. It lists all conferences where the British Library has received the proceedings. The Library in turn indexes conference proceedings on its Inside database.

There are also some websites that notify you of forthcoming conferences, a particularly useful site is at **http://www.nlm.nih.gov/services/ medmeet.html**.

Vital statistics

The list below shows some of the more useful publications that can help with statistical enquiries.

- The Stationery Office published the *Annual Abstract of Statistics* which is compiled by the Office of National Statistics in London. This publication covers more than health statistics but gives a good overview of the UK in numbers and covers about 10 years of data so comparisons can be made.

- The Office of National Statistics (ONS) formerly the Office of Population Censuses and Surveys (OPCS) produces a lot of useful health information much of which is available through its website at **http://www.ons.gov.uk**. Much of the material is derived from the national registration system for births and deaths and the ONS's systems for notification of congenital abnormalities and infectious diseases. It also carries out work on behalf of the Department of Health and the Health Development Agency (formerly the Health Education Authority).

- The Department of Health produces *On the State of the Public Health* which is the annual report of the Chief Medical Officer. It gives some statistical data but is particularly useful for topics of current interest.

- The World Health Organization has published its *World Health Statistics Annual* each year since 1952. It contains life tables, morbidity and mortality rates for most countries of the world in both English and French. The WHO website gives users access to its Statistical Information Service (WHOSIS) and is available at **http://www.who.int**.

- *Medistat: World Medical Market Analysis*. MDIS Publications, Chichester is a very useful and interesting publication and is available as a loose-leaf print version which is regularly updated or as a CD-ROM. It lists details of the health expenditure as GDP, hospital addresses, medical device companies and pharmaceutical companies for all countries of the world. A really useful directory.

Pharmaceutical literature

The tracking down of information in the pharmaceutical field is a whole topic in itself. Some of the more useful directories and information sources are given below.

- The most useful pharmacopoeia is *Martindale, the Extra Pharmacopoeia*, 31st ed, edited by: James E.F. Reynolds, deputy editor: Kathleen Parfitt, assistant editors: Anne V. Parsons, Sean C. Sweetman, Royal Pharmaceutical Society, London. 1996. Martindale contains chapters on the major drug types that give a general description of the drug type followed by details of each drug including trade names, dosage, adverse effects and references. *Martindale* is available on CD-ROM and searchable online through The Dialog Corporation.

- The *British Pharmacopoeia 2000* (now with accompanying CD-ROM). The Stationery Office, London. 2000. This is the accepted legal standard in Britain and the Commonwealth for the drugs published in it. The standards laid down in the *European Pharmacopoeia* are largely becoming the standards in Britain.

- The *British Herbal Pharmacopoeia*, 4th ed, British Herbal Medicine Association, 1996. This is the herbal equivalent of the British Pharmacopoeia as the *British Homeopathic Pharmacopoeia*, 2nd ed, British Association of Homeopathic Manufacturers, Rutland, 1999 is the homeopathic equivalent.

- The Association of British Pharmaceutical Industries produce the *Compendium of Data Sheets and Summaries of Product Characteristics* (a.k.a the *Data Sheet Compendium*) each year which is sent free to practitioners and pharmacists. It contains text for the summaries of product descriptions, approved by the Medicines Agency, for most of the medicines available in the

UK. A new electronic version is available on the Web at **http://emc. vhn.net**. Users need to register to use the site but there are no charges for doing this.

- The most frequently consulted drug text is probably the *British National Formulary* which is published every six months and which most doctors carry around with them in their pockets. It is produced jointly by the Royal Pharmaceutical Society and the British Medical Association and is also available as the electronic BNF (e-BNF) on CD-ROM with the Drug and Therapeutic Bulletin and the MeReC Bulletin which lists new medicines.

- The *Monthly Index of Medical Specialities (MIMS)* is written by independent experts and is designed as a prescribing guide for general practitioners. Information is written in a strictly controlled format which includes prescription only medicine as well as some over the counter products if they have been approved by the Advisory Committee on Borderline Substances. A version is now available on CD-ROM.

- The *Merck Index: an Encyclopedia of Chemicals, Drugs, and Biologicals*, edited by Susan Budavari, 12th ed. Merck Research Laboratories, Whitehouse Station, N.J. 1996, also available as a CD-ROM version with additional monographs, contains a series of monographs on drugs and other biological substances. It is now available as an online database through The DIALOG Corporation and STN (another European host) covering some 10,000 records. Each record contains systematic, generic, trivial and product names for a compound plus its CAS Registry number, manufacturer and distributor and toxicity and usage. It has bibliographic citations for each compound where these are relevant.

- For adverse effects of drugs the best information can be found in both *Meyler's Side Effects of Drugs, Excerpta Medica*, Amsterdam and Oxford, 1975 and *Side Effects of Drugs Annual* edited by M.N.G. Dukes et al. These two combined form the database SEDBASE which is available online from Datastar and DIALOG and are complete up to 1995. It covers information on more than 50,000 drug side effects and over 4,000 drug interactions.

- The *Chemist and Druggist* is a monthly publication which is aimed at pharmacists and lists both drugs and other materials available from pharmacists with details of their manufacturers and suppliers. It is useful for tracking down brand names and the manufacturer who supplies them.

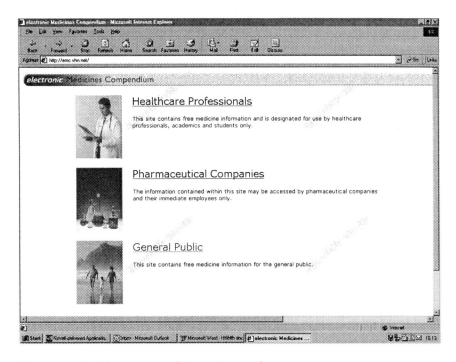

Figure 1 The Electronic Medicines Compendium

Chapter 2.   Electronic Resources

Finding published materials

In the previous chapter we have discussed how to find book material and where
the major collections are housed. This chapter aims to look at the major source of
information to support health care and which is mainly found in the journal
literature.

The journal literature

A journal or serial or periodical publication may be defined as a publication
issued in successive parts which is planned to continue indefinitely. Works such as
Annual Reviews and the *Yearbook* series are periodicals whereas conference
proceedings and technical reports are not considered as such. A health library will
contain many periodicals as they are the primary means of reporting research and
are published on a very rapid turnaround – weekly, monthly or quarterly. A good
health library can be judged on the number of journals that it holds as opposed
to textbooks or reference works. Much of the library budget will go on journals
and various methods for storing them.

It is difficult to ascertain the number of health-related journals today although
Wyatt in *The Lancet* in 1991 estimated that there were then about 32,000
compared to just 1,654 in 1912. This number has been modified downwards
recently as journals are both created and 'die'. However, it is undeniable that the
health literature has exploded exponentially and this has led to the major problem
of 'information overload' in the health profession.

As mentioned in the first chapter, there are two types of periodical literature –
the primary journals such as *The Lancet* and the *British Medical Journal* and the
secondary which includes abstracting journals and indexes such as *Index Medicus*.
Some authors also refer to tertiary journals which they classify as those journals
containing reviews such as the *Annual Review of Biochemistry*.

Search tools

To access this vast wealth of health information has become easier over the last 30
years with the advent of computer searching. To track the literature before this
time, you will need to turn to the printed abstracting and indexing journals, some
of which are listed here.

Printed abstracting and indexing journals

Most of the printed indexes and abstracts are now available electronically but for searching of the literature before the 1960s you will usually need to use the printed versions of these electronic databases. Actually tracking down printed indexes can also be hard work as many libraries are now discarding print in favour of electronic access.

Surgeon General's Catalogue

The United States of America produce the most important indexes of the medical literature. The first of these was the *Index-catalogue of the Surgeon General's Office* which was conceived by John Shaw Billings, a distinguished American librarian. He produced a specimen catalogue in 1876 which was well received and so he proceeded with the Index-catalogue. The first volume appeared in 1880 and publication continued annually with each volume covering a different letter of the alphabet. When the alphabet was completed a new series was begun again working through the literature and picking up new material which had been received by the library. Publication ceased in the middle of the fourth series owing to its inability to cope with the huge growth in the medical literature. A further drawback was that due to the alphabetical nature of the publication, some material might wait 20 years before getting onto the list.

The volumes that are available are:

- 1st Series: Vol 1-16   1880-1895

- 2nd Series: Vol 1-21   1896-1916

- 3rd Series: Vol 1-10   1918-1932

- 4th Series: Vol 1-11 (A-Mn)   1936-1955

A fifth series containing selected books appeared in 3 vols 1959-1961. Various supplementary catalogues have been released since and the *NLM Current Catalogue* was the latest version of this vast undertaking. Although it only lists the holdings of the Surgeon General's Library (later the National Library of Medicine) people consider it to be a complete list of the medical literature from the advent of printing to the middle of the 20th century. It should be remembered however that many books did not appear till years after they were printed or were included when the library bought them, also Billings was fairly selective as to which periodical literature should be included.

In 1966 the NLM brought out its *NLM Current Catalogue Cumulations*. However, in 1993 this ceased publication and all the catalogues became electronically searchable.

Index Medicus

Index Medicus has had a chequered career being produced in various editions by the National Library of Medicine and the American Medical Association at various times in its life. It has also changed its name to *Quarterly Cumulative Index Medicus* and to *Current List of Medical Literature* during its lifetime to satisfy the demand for up-to-date listings of the periodical literature. In January 1960 the *Current List* was replaced by *Index Medicus* which was published monthly and cumulated annually. Currently *Index Medicus* is produced by the National Library of Medicine, covers about 4,000 titles and cumulates annually into 14 volumes which are classified by author and subject using the *MeSH* subject headings. For some years in the '80s and '90s there was an *Abridged Index Medicus* which contained the 120 most popular medical journals but this has since ceased publication. *Index Medicus* is perhaps best known as the printed version of the Medline database.

The National Library of Medicine also produces a series of *Current Bibliographies in Medicine* which cover a number of up to the minute topics (i.e. telemedicine). These are available free from the Web via the NLM home page at **http:// www.nlm.nih.gov.**

Current Contents

Current Contents is produced by the Institute for Scientific Information and is a weekly current awareness tool consisting of reproductions of the contents pages of about 7,000 journals and some books. The three of most interest in the health field are *Current Contents: Life Sciences* (1,379 titles), *Current Contents: Clinical Medicine* (1,083 titles) and *Current Contents: Social and Behavioral Sciences* (1,596 titles). There is some overlap between the titles. Each issues contains a selective list of book series, reviews and proceedings as well as list of journals, a subject index and the addresses of the first author of each article appearing. An updated list of the journals covered is produced twice a year.

Science Citation Index

Also produced by the Institute for Scientific Information (ISI), *Science Citation Index* and *Social Science Citation Index*, work in a slightly different way to other indexing and abstracting services. Eugene Garfield who started ISI, defines a citation index as 'an ordered list of references (cited works) in which each reference is followed by a list of the sources (citing works) which cite it'. Its main purpose is to lead the searcher from a key paper to others which have referred to that key paper, assuming that they will be relevant. It is published every 2 months with annual cumulations.

Excerpta Medica

Excerpta Medica Foundation and its associate, the publisher Elsevier, also publish a series of monthly or twice monthly printed bibliographies on selected medical topics. These are also available as the EMBASE database.

Other bibliographies

There are also many specialised published bibliographic listings for particular areas in health and medicine. The British Library produces a series called *Healthcare Updates* which are either monthly or quarterly and cover topics from asthma to learning disabilities. These are inexpensive to subscribe to but keep health care professionals up to date with developments.

Electronic resources – Medline

Medline is possibly the most famous medical bibliography in the world. Started in 1966 by the National Library of Medicine, it was the electronic version of *Index Medicus* and was indexed using *MeSH* headings which allowed for very controlled searching at the time. Techniques for accessing Medline have changed over the years. Originally tapes were supplied by the NLM and these were run on the host countries' computers – the host had to be a government department, the British Library took on this role in the UK and made Medline available via their BLAISE system. This changed in the '70s and '80s when a dial up 'online' service direct to the NLM was offered and other hosts services were allowed to hold Medline, again in the late '80s access via CD-ROM became popular and in 1997 the NLM offered MEDLINE free on the Internet via PubMed and Internet Grateful Med. MEDLINE, as the electronic version of *Index Medicus*, covers about 4,000 journals and these remain roughly constant, with new journals being taken on and old ones dropped. The Board of Regents of the NLM decide on which titles should be included in MEDLINE using various criteria such as timeliness and whether the journal is peer-reviewed. It should be noted, as it is a constant source of confusion, that Medline is the database and PubMed, OVID, SilverPlatter and EBSCO etc. are just various methods of accessing Medline.

Although the next section is about the various ways of searching MEDLINE, it applies equally to the other electronic databases listed.

Medline on CD-ROM – OVID and SILVERPLATTER and the rest

There are two main suppliers of CD-ROM versions of Medline in the UK. These are SilverPlatter and OVID. SilverPlatter is the older of the two companies

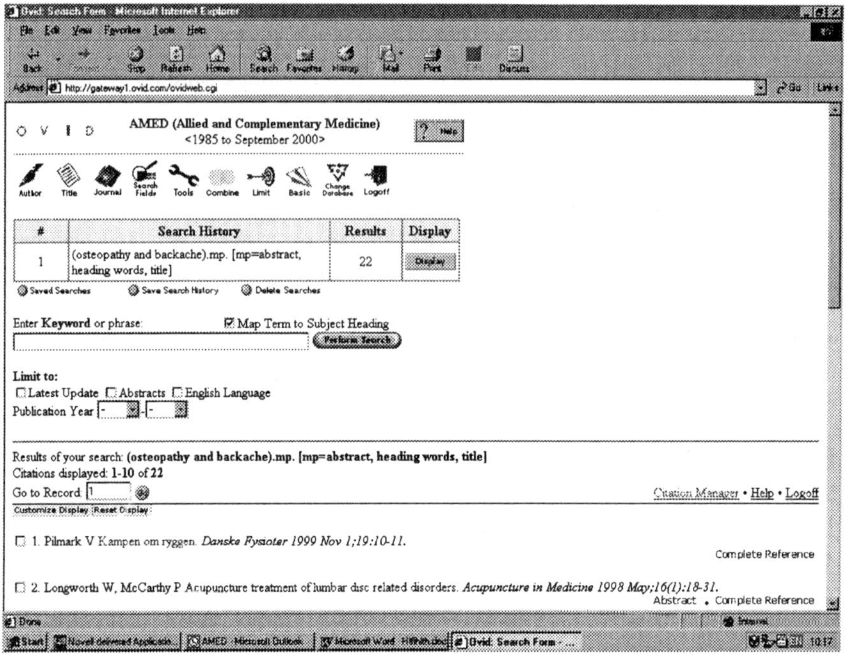

Figure 2 The OVID Web interface

and traditionally it would appear that NHS Libraries favour OVID whilst higher education libraries favour SilverPlatter, although with consortium deals becoming the norm, that may change. Both offer very similar facilities but search in slightly different ways. CD-ROM has not yet been superseded by Internet versions even with 'free' MEDLINE on the Internet. Reasons for this vary but libraries have invested in the infrastructure of CD-ROM, buying jukeboxes and RAID disk arrays and many librarians prefer the interface of the CD-ROM to that on the Internet.

A disadvantage of CD-ROM is its currency. Most databases on CD-ROM are updated monthly but can still run several months behind, most large databases also require more than one CD-ROM to contain them and updating on a regular basis can be difficult and time consuming. Online access through a host system or the Internet can make this a lot easier and the databases supplied this way tend to be much more up to date.

Two other suppliers who are also building a following in UK health libraries are EBSCO and Aries Knowledge Finder, although these systems tend to be more prevalent in the US.

12

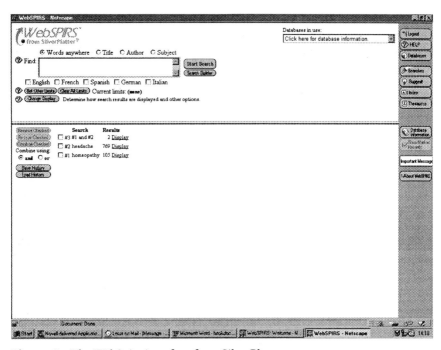

Figure 3 The WebSpirs interface from SilverPlatter

EBSCO has Comprehensive Medline on CD-ROM as well as a number of other biomedical databases but many libraries will access databases through the EBSCOHost system on the Web. Aries Knowledge Finder also has some sites in the UK.

Both versions offer different search interfaces to MEDLINE and the other databases they provide. Each has their own proponents – OVID has been favoured by many librarians because of its automatic mapping facility although SilverPlatter also offers this in a slightly different form.

On both systems you are presented with a search box into which you type your terms.

When you type in a search term, OVID maps to what it considers is the most appropriate *MeSH* heading for MEDLINE, whereas SilverPlatter does the same through the 'suggest' button. Both versions have a complete copy of *MeSH* built in to the system (this is also true for the Internet versions), so the most appropriate *MeSH* term can be chosen. Both will allow you to combine search terms using the number of the search statement and then view your results in a variety of formats either short format without abstract or long with abstract and *MeSH* headings. A printing or downloading facility is also offered but may depend on what the Library holding the database will allow you to do.

Internet – PubMed and Internet Grateful Med

Since June 1997, Medline and the other NLM databases have been made freely available on the Internet. PubMed (**http://www.ncbi.nlm.nih.gov:80/ entrez/query.fcgi**) is the National Library of Medicine's search service that provides access to over 11 million citations in MEDLINE, PreMEDLINE, and other related databases, with links to participating online journals. PubMed is aimed at the novice searcher although new features have been added to allow complex Boolean searches. Internet Grateful Med is another interface for Medline and the other NLM databases. This allows more complex searches and the ability to use the Unified Medical Language System (UMLS) to match search terms to *MeSH* headings.

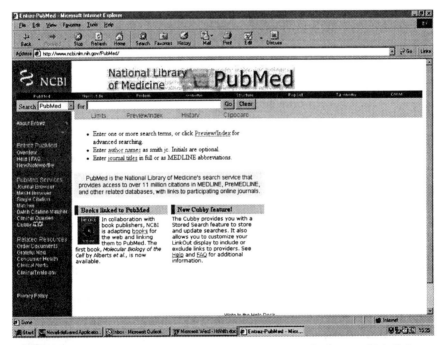

Figure 4 The PubMed search interface from the National Library of Medicine

Other free Internet providers

There are a number of other Web-based hosts that offer Medline and various other NLM databases free of charge, OMNI (*see* below) offers a listing of these on their website. These include:

- **Healthworks (http://www.healthworks.co.uk)** is a UK based company that offers free Medline and a daily news feed as well as other useful links and information.

- **BioMedNet (http://www.bmn.com)** is owned by Elsevier Science and is the website for biological medical researchers. BioMedNet allows you to search Medline and the Swiss-Prot database (a protein sequence database) which is free, and members can search all of BioMedNet without charge. There is also a daily news update feature and *HMS Beagle* which is a free magazine. Links to the British Library Document Supply Centre allow you to order documents at a cost and viewing full-text articles from publishers often requires payment or a subscription.

Medline and online hosts

Although searching MEDLINE and other databases on online hosts using a text-based command language is becoming less popular, they are still a way of accessing a large number of databases and allow cross database searching and de-duplication of results. The rise of the Internet has resulted in many of the traditional online hosts offering a Web interface to search the databases that they make available.

Two of the main online hosts are Datastar and Dialog which are both owned by The Dialog Corporation (**http://www.dialog.com**) – DataStar is a European host whilst Dialog is mainly US based, but with the advent of the Web, these geographical limitations are seen as meaningless. Other European hosts include the German host DIMDI (Deutsches Institut für Medizinische Dokumentation und Information) which makes a large number of databases available and is searchable using a Web interface and STN, offering mainly chemical databases.

DIMDI is part of the European Information Network Services (EINS – **http://www.eins.org**) which is a consortium of European hosts, which make a wide range of scientific databases available to researchers. None of these hosts are free and all attract a charge for searching, so some competency in searching and preparation before actually 'going online' is necessary to keep down costs.

The CD-ROM providers – OVID, SilverPlatter, EBSCO and Aries also provide Web access to their databases on a subscription basis with links to document supply features and to full text electronic journals where they are available. OVID also provides the 'Core Biomedical Collection' of full text electronic journals which are some of the most popular journals made available to subscribers.

Another service that is becoming more popular is HCN's MIRON system which provides Internet access to many biomedical databases including Medline, CINAHL and AMED.

Other providers of electronic health databases

- **EMBASE** is produced by Elsevier Scientific Publications and is the electronic version of the Excerpta Medica published abstracts on various topics (mentioned in the previous section). EMBASE also has a thesaurus of terms called EMTREE which is also available as a separate paper publication. EMBASE indexes about the same number of journals as MEDLINE, 3,800, but there is only about 30-40% overlap and EMBASE is particularly strong in the pharmaceutical area. It is really the other major medical bibliography and for a really complete search should be searched alongside MEDLINE. It is not as common in libraries as MEDLINE although there are moves in place, with consortium buying, to rectify the situation. It is available on CD-ROM and the Internet from OVID, SilverPlatter and EBSCO.

- **The British Nursing Index** is produced by the Royal College of Nursing and the University of Bournemouth with Poole Hospital NHS Trust. It indexes journal articles from all the major British nursing and midwifery titles and other English language titles, over 200 journals in total. The topics covered include all aspects of nursing and some information on alternative therapies. It is available on CD-ROM from SilverPlatter and by password on the Internet (**www.bni.org.uk**).

- **The Cumulative Index of Nursing and Allied Health Literature** (CINAHL) is produced by CINAHL Information Systems in Glendale, California. It covers the nursing and allied health disciplines which include the therapies such as physiotherapy and occupational therapy as well as laboratory technology and nutrition. It indexes more than 1,100 journals. It also includes books and pamphlets, dissertations, proceedings, standards and software. Original documents include drug records, accreditation, legal cases and clinical innovation. Some selected full text material is also included. The database is available from a number of suppliers, online through DIALOG and DataStar and on CD-ROM through OVID, SilverPlatter and EBSCO.

- **The Health Management Information Consortium** (HMIC) covers health management information both in the UK and internationally. It is a collection of three bibliographic databases – The Department of Health's database which is also available separately as DHData on DataStar, the Kings Fund database and HELMIS, formerly produced by the Nuffield Institute for Health but no longer available. The CD-ROM and Web version are available from SilverPlatter.

- **Allied and Complementary Medicine database** (AMED) is produced by the British Library's Health Care Information Service and covers the areas of Complementary Medicine, Physiotherapy, Occupational Therapy, Rehabilitation Medicine, Palliative Care, Podiatry and Speech and Language Therapy. Its coverage extends back to 1985, when the database was started due to the lack of coverage of these topics on MEDLINE. It has a thesaurus of terms based on *MeSH* and since 1993 has had abstracts. It is available as print, and on CD-ROM through SilverPlatter and OVID as well as on the Web via EBSCOMed.

- **Applied Social Science Index and Abstracts** (ASSIA) covers the areas of the social sciences which includes geriatrics, child abuse and NHS reforms and management. They index about 550 journals and each record includes a short abstract. It is available on DIALOG and DataStar and the producer, Bowker-Saur produces its own CD-ROM version.

- **PsycINFO and PsycLIT**. The PsycINFO database corresponds to the printed 'Psychological Abstracts' produced by the American Psychological Association and covers the international literature on psychology and psychiatry from 1887. It indexes more than 1,400 international journals and about 57,000 references are added annually. PsycINFO is available online through DataStar, DIALOG and DIMDI but subsets are available on CD-ROM. PsycLIT is a subset dealing with the academic and professional literature on psychology and is available via OVID, SilverPlatter and EBSCO Publishing. CLINPsyc is also a subset dealing with medical and clinical psychology.

These are probably the major databases that will be available in any health library but that is far from the total amount of specialised data available to the researcher or health care professional. A couple of other databases may be worth mentioning for more in-depth searching.

- **The Health Economic Evaluations Database** (HEED) is produced by the Office for Health Economics and contains information on cost effectiveness of medicine and other treatments. It contains information on more than 15,000 economic evaluations, over half of which have been reviewed by a panel of experts. About 200 fully reviewed articles are added each month which are selected from online databases and the leading journals but some unpublished material is also included. It is available for a yearly subscription.

- **NHS Health Database.** The database contains three modules which can be used together or separately. One module contains Health Authority commissioning plans, public health reports and service reviews. The Primary Care Group module contains details from PCG's and the 'Provider' module contains Trust annual reports and service plans. The database is available on CD-ROM and is produced by Blackwell Masters Ltd and the NHS Confederation.

- **OECD Health Data** is a useful tool for comparing health data between OECD member countries. It includes information such as health status, financing, resources and the market. You can sample the data at – **www. oecd.org/els/health/software**. It is available as a CD-ROM on subscription.

The NLM also produces a number of bibliographic databases, other than Medline, on specific topics such as HIV/AIDS (Aidsline) and cancer (Cancerlit). A list of these databases is available from the NLM Website (**www.nlm.nih.gov**) and they are currently searchable through Internet Grateful Med (**http://igm. nlm.nih.gov**). Plans for amalgamation of all of these databases into one huge database are under way and this database will be searchable using the PubMed interface. Many are currently available through online hosts such as DIALOG and DIMDI and CD-ROMs exist of some of the more useful ones.

Toxicology databases

It is worth mentioning two sources for toxicology information as they are both provided by the National Library of Medicine. TOXLINE is the bibliographic database which includes references going back to 1965 with some older key references. It contains references gleaned from Medline, BIOSIS and several US Government publications from agencies such as NIOSH (National Institute of Occupational Safety and Health) and the EPA (Environmental Protection Agency). The other collection of databases is called TOXNET, which contains pure data about the toxicity levels of chemical and biological substances. TOXLINE and the constituent databases of TOXNET are available through various online hosts such as Dialog and DIMDI. They are both available on the Web through the NLM's Specialized Information Services home page (**http://sis.nlm.nih.gov/tehip.cfm**) and TOXLINE can be subscribed to on a SilverPlatter CD-ROM.

The Internet

Many users see the Internet as replacing libraries completely. They seem to believe that everything is on the Web, so why should they need to look elsewhere? Although it is true that much information is now on the Internet and that there is probably a website on most subjects now – a lot of the information is of dubious quality and some is downright dangerous. A recent goal of health librarians and some health care professionals is to try to bring some sort of quality criteria to the Web. Other projects such as DISCERN are trying to teach consumers the value of critical appraisal applied to websites. Some of the sites mentioned below are heavily involved in listing quality health sites but as the Web changes from day to day, it would be impossible to list all sites:

- **Organising Medical Networked Information** (OMNI) (**www.omni. ac.uk**) was started as one of the e-lib (electronic library) projects by the academic sector funded by the Joint Information Steering Committee (JISC). Its remit was to locate and list quality medical sites on the Internet with an emphasis on UK sites. Over the years it has performed this task using a set of quality criteria and volunteer librarians to locate sites and then write short descriptors of the site plus a link to the site. Currently there are over 4,000 resources on OMNI which are searchable using a very simple interface or browsable using the NLM classification scheme or a system based on the UMLS system. OMNI is now part of the larger BIOME (**www.biome.ac.uk**) project which is looking to provide a gateway to Web resources in the life sciences sector.

- **Medical Matrix** (**www.medmatrix.org**) was founded by Gary Malet in the US and is a gateway site to medical and health-related resources on the Internet. It contains a very large collection of links to sites of interest and the categories include literature, directories as well as clinical sites.

- **Health on the Net** (HON) (**www.hon.ch**) is based in Geneva and is designed to realise the benefits of the Internet for health care. It contains information of use to the health care professional and has a search engine called MedHunt which helps track down websites. It indexes sites both manually and automatically and the HON foundation has initiated a Code of Conduct for health-related websites.

Keeping up to date

For keeping really current in your subject, you need to use a 'current awareness service'. These databases are not indexed in great depth as currency is their main aim and indexing of articles takes time. Usually you can search by a keyword in the title or by author or journal title. Current Contents is also available in a printed version.

- **Infotrieve (http://www3.infotrieve.com/medline/infotrieve)** offer a free Web-based service for current awareness using the Medline database. You can set up your search using an easy intuitive Web form and the search is run every time the database is updated. It is easy to define a highly sophisticated search and to use such refinements as limits and age groups

- **Mindit (http://mindit.netmind.com)** is a free service which alerts you every time a website that you are interested in is changed. It could be useful on sites that give details of grants etc. An e-mail arrives every time the sites you choose are updated.

- **Inside (http://www.bl.uk/inside)** is the British Library's current awareness product. 21,000 of the most requested journals have their contents pages keyed into a database which is updated regularly. The database is particularly strong on the science, technology and medical areas and journals such as the *British Medical Journal* are added to the database within a couple of days of receipt. In addition to the searching capabilities, you can also order documents from the British Library's collection at a cost which includes a copyright fee. *INSIDE Alerts* offers a selected profile of journal titles to be run against the Inside database and the contents pages of those journals to be delivered directly to the user's e-mail address.

- **Current Contents** is also available electronically as a disk or online through the DataStar and Dialog host systems. Both OVID and SilverPlatter make a CD-ROM version available. Current Contents is also available through the ISI's Web of Science.

- **Web of Science (http://www.isinet.com)** is the Internet version of the citation indexes produced by ISI – *see* Science Citation Index in the previous section. Web of Science contains the following databases:

  - Science Citation Index Expanded with Cited References and Author Abstracts (1981-);

  - Social Sciences Citation Index Expanded with Cited References and Author Abstracts (1981-);

  - Arts & Humanities Citation Index with Cited References (1981-).

It also gives access to The Index to Scientific and Technical Proceeding (ISTP) from 1990 which indexes the published literature of the most significant conferences, symposia, seminars, colloquia workshops and conventions in a wide range of disciplines in science and technology.

In addition other products are available for an extra charge, these include Current Content Connect (CCC) which is a current awareness database that includes information in the fields of science, social science, technology and arts and humanities. The latest version features profile-based alerting that gives users the ability to create and manage a set number of alerts that will run against the Current Contents data. Once a week, the results are automatically forwarded to a specified e-mail address.

The Current Contents titles included are:

- Life Sciences with Author Abstracts,

- Clinical Medicine with Author Abstracts,

- Agriculture, Biology & Environmental Sciences with Author Abstracts,

- Engineering, Computing & Technology with Author Abstracts,

- Physical, Chemical & Earth Sciences with Author Abstracts,

- Social & Behavioral Sciences with Author Abstracts,

- Arts & Humanities (no Author Abstracts available).

Also on Web of Science are the Journal Citation Reports (JCR) which are a comprehensive, and unique resource for journal evaluation, using citation data drawn from over 8,400 scholarly and technical journals worldwide. Coverage is both multidisciplinary and international, and incorporates journals from over 3,000 publishers in 60 nations.

The JCR is the only source of citation data on journals, and includes virtually all specialties in the areas of science, technology, and the social sciences. JCR Web shows the relationship between citing and cited journals. JCR Web is available annually in two editions:

- Science Edition which contains data from roughly 5,000 journals in the areas of science and technology.

- Social Sciences Edition which contains data from roughly 1,500 journals in the social sciences.

Due to an agreement with CHEST, which purchases databases and software for the Higher Education sector in the UK, you will find Web of Science in most university libraries and some of the larger NHS Trust libraries.

21

Patient information

It is perhaps worth mentioning a couple of useful sites for information aimed at patients rather than health care professionals. You will find that many NHS libraries already provide access to patients and have a range of materials for their use.

- **Helpbox** is produced by the Help for Health Trust in Winchester. It is a computerised database which is made available on disk and runs under the Microsoft Windows operating system. It contains three files and can be edited to add local information. The data contained includes self-help group addresses, leaflets and books.

- **Medline Plus (http://medlineplus.gov)** is another database available from the National Library of Medicine. It provides access to extensive information about specific diseases and conditions and also has links to consumer health information from the National Institutes of Health, dictionaries, lists of hospitals and physicians, health information in Spanish and other languages, and clinical trials.

- **Healthfinder (http://www.healthfinder.gov)** is a free gateway to consumer health and human services information developed by the US Department of Health and Human Services. It contains selected online publications, clearing houses, databases, websites, and support and self-help groups, as well as the government agencies and not-for-profit organisations that produce information for the public. It was launched in April 1997 and served Internet users over 1.7 million times in its first year online.

- **NHS Direct Online (http://www.nhsdirect.nhs.uk)** is the Web version of the NHS Direct telephone triage service. It makes information available for patients about the NHS as well as simple guides to conditions and treatments which can be administered at home.

Other similar services are offered by doctors.net (**www.doctors.net**), Surgery Door (**http://www.surgerydoor.co.uk**) and NetDoctor, which is an independent medical site, at **http://www.netdoctor.co.uk**.

Searching techniques

This can only be a basic guide to searching electronic databases – your local librarian should be able to help with the more detailed searching techniques that can be used with each database. As a start you will find that the best way to search is to break down your query into its separate topics. The examples given below can be run on most systems whether CD-ROM, online or on the Net – the only difference would be the look of the interface.

You will find that most of the database interfaces now run under a graphical user interface (GUI) such as Microsoft Windows or the Apple Macintosh interface depending on which system your library favours. The search screen will therefore have a list of commands on a menu bar across the top of the screen and a search box where you can enter your search terms. Under this on the screen will be some sort of results box which will tell you how many items you have retrieved for each term you entered and these will be given a 'search statement' number i.e.

1: Osteopathy	2000
2: Backache	500
3: 1 & 2	10

In the example above we have looked for the use of osteopathy in backache. We have typed in osteopathy and backache and the system has assigned the search statement numbers 1 and 2 to the two search terms. The system has then combined the two terms to bring up a third result with both terms included. This introduces the concept of Boolean logic which you may hear librarians talking about. The three statements most commonly used are AND, OR, NOT – and these can be used to give differing results in a search i.e. OSTEOPATHY and BACKACHE would find articles which include both the terms Osteopathy and Backache. OSTEOPATHY or BACKACHE would retrieve more articles as it is looking for the two terms and so would retrieve articles containing the word Osteopathy or the word Backache. OSTEOPATHY not BACKACHE would retrieve articles about Osteopathy but not where the word Backache appears.

By assigning search statement numbers, the user can build up complicated searches i.e. 1 and 2 not 3 without having to type the terms in again which can be useful when you get onto your 25th search term!

The user can also use brackets to build even more complicated search statements i.e. (OSTEOPATHY or ACUPUNCTURE) not (BACKACHE or ASTHMA) would retrieve terms which were on Osteopathy or Acupuncture but not where those articles contained the words Asthma or Backache.

It should be noted that all systems will have a series of stopwords which you should avoid using in your searches. These are fairly common and consist of words such as 'and', 'the' and 'but'.

Most systems will also allow you to impose limits to your search. These include:

- Human or Animal

- Age ranges – i.e. 0-10, 10-20 or adolescent, elderly, middle aged

- Publication type – i.e. review, guideline, etc.

- Language of publication i.e. English or French, etc.

- Date ranges – i.e. 1990-1999

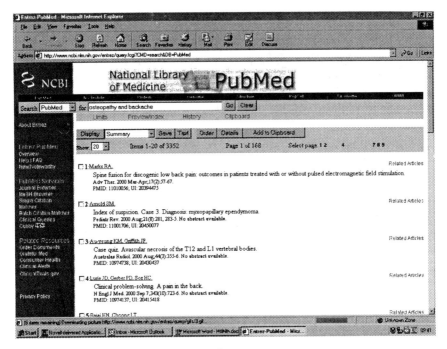

Figure 5 A Boolean search in PubMed

These can be useful if you retrieve too many references in the first place. Age ranges are preferred if searching for articles about the elderly – for instance doing a search on the word 'aged' would retrieve articles with titles including the word aged i.e. patients aged between 10 and 20. Publication type can be useful for an overview of a subject i.e. if you are searching for Asthma and retrieve thousands of references by using the 'review' publication type you will retrieve only articles that are reviews of the topic. It is also worth remembering that certain publications only specialise in reviews i.e. the *Annual Reviews* series or the *'Clinics of North America'* series. It is also worth remembering that reviews can also be biased towards the author's point of view so more than one review may be worth retrieving. A course on 'critical appraisal' skills might be useful if you are going to be retrieving a lot of literature for a project.

Truncation is also a useful tool for searching i.e. CHILD$ would retrieve child or children – the $ symbol just substitutes a number of letters. The $, hash or : signs are popular and used in many systems – the help files for the system should be able to guide you as to the correct symbol. It is also worth noting that too much truncation can lead to interesting results so that CH$ would retrieve child or children but also chilli, chestnut etc.

24

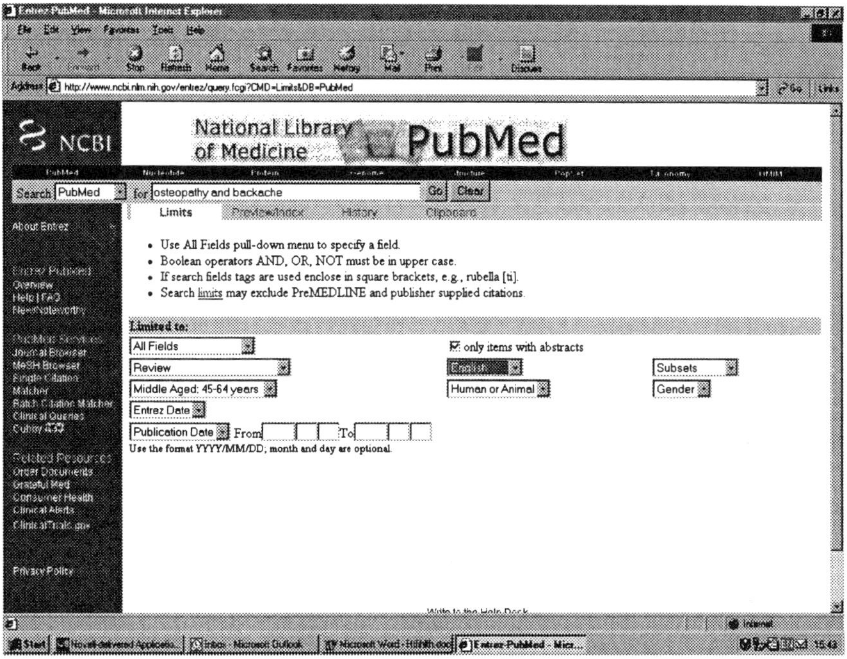

Figure 6 The limit feature in PubMed

MEDLINE also provides 'subheadings' which are listed in the printed *MeSH* and also on most of the electronic versions of the database. Subheadings are applied to each section of *MeSH* for instance the C LIST which is the section for General Diseases includes the following:

BL /blood
CF /cerebrospinal fluid
CI /chemical industry
CL /classification
CN /congenital
CO /complications
DH /diet therapy
DI /diagnosis
DT /drug therapy
EC /economics
EH /ethnology
EM /embryology
EN /enzymology
EP /epidemiology

25

ET /etiology
GE /genetics
HI /history
IM /immunology
ME /metabolism
MI /microbiology
MO /mortality
NU /nursing
PA /pathology
PC /prevention
PP /physiopathology
PS /parasitology
PX /psychology
RA /radiography
RH /rehabilitation
RI /radionuclide
RT /radiotherapy
SU /surgery
TH /therapy
UR /urine
US /ultrasonography
VE /veterinary
VI /virology

The two letter tag can be added to your search term as a sort of qualifier, so drug terms will allow you to add 'AE' for adverse effects or 'PO' for poisoning. As a practical example in Internet Grateful Med (**http://igm.nlm.nih.gov**) when you type a term into one of the search boxes and click on the 'find related' button, the browser takes you to the most appropriate *MeSH* term. If you select this in the tick box, the system then allows you to assign a subheading to make that search more specific and transfers the search term back to the search screen.

Theses and dissertations

British Reports, Translations and Theses (BRTT) is published monthly with a microfiche index of cumulated keyterms, authors and report numbers which is supplied quarterly and is available on subscription. Based on the holdings of the National Reports Collection at the British Library Document Supply Centre, BRTT is a listing of newly published reports, technical papers and dissertations produced by non-commercial publishers such as research institutions, private and public sector organisations, charities, and action groups. English translations of foreign language reports and doctoral theses are also included. All subject areas are covered.

The *Index to Theses Accepted for Higher Degrees by the Universities of Great Britain and Ireland* has been available as a print subscription for a number of years and was originally produced by Aslib (The Association of Libraries and Information Bureaux). However, the Index is now available on the Web at **http://www. theses.com/**. The database covers theses accepted from 1970 to 1999 covering all of volumes 21 to 48 and parts 1 to 3 of volume 49 of the equivalent print publication *Index to Theses*.

Finding 'grey' literature including official publications

'Grey' literature is usually classified as that material that does not have an ISBN or ISSN. It usually includes technical reports, official publications and report materials. It also can contain a lot of useful information including statistics and research findings but is always difficult to track down in catalogues. It can also be difficult to collect unless the publisher deposits the publication with a legal deposit library. One database that tries to list grey literature is SIGLE.

- **System for Information on Grey Literature in Europe** (SIGLE) is produced by the EAGLE consortium; the British Library is the UK partner and covers grey literature from 1980 to date. It provides access to records for reports and other grey literature in all subject areas produced in Europe. The database contains records from nine European countries, along with some of the R&D material produced by the Commission of the European Communities. The majority of material cited is in English, and that indicated as being held at the British Library Document Supply Centre can be ordered online; many documents cited as being from other sources may also be available from DSC. The file is updated monthly and is available currently online on BLAISE-LINE from the BL and on CD-ROM from SilverPlatter.

For tracking down official publications in the health field, the following two sites are a mine of information and are a good place to start.

- **The Stationery Office (http://www.official-documents.co.uk)** (formerly Her Majesty's Stationery Office – HMSO) has a very comprehensive website which lists all available government publications. They also publish daily, weekly and monthly lists of government publications in print to which some health libraries will subscribe.

- **The Department of Health (http://www.doh.gov.uk)** site has grown in importance and is now one of the major ways for finding out about the DOH, the NHS and the publications that they produce. Two catalogues of publications, COIN and POINT list circulars and publications respectively. A subject search however is not recommended as the whole site is searched, so you need to be able to start from a point where you know the circular number or the publication title. However, it is a useful tool for tracking down and printing copies of DOH circulars.

Chapter 3.   Other Health Libraries

The Directory of Medical and Health Care libraries in the United Kingdom and the Republic of Ireland published by the Library Association and now in its 8th edition and the *Guide to Libraries and Information Sources in Medicine and Health Care*, edited by Peter Dale, 3rd edition published by the British Library, provide details of most of the health care libraries in the UK. Similar lists exist for libraries in North America and the rest of the world.

The following are some of the major health collections which can be accessed in the UK and one of the major international collections at the National Library of Medicine in Washington D.C.

The British Library
96 Euston Road, London NW1 2DB. Tel: 020 7412 7288
(**http://www.bl.uk**)

The British Library is the national library of the UK and is a general library situated on three sites. The British Library is a legal deposit library and receives all material published in the United Kingdom – it does not, as popular rumour has it, have every book ever published.

The London reading rooms are at St Pancras and Colindale (the Newspaper Library) and the Document Supply Centre is in Boston Spa in Yorkshire. The collections of the British Library are listed on OPAC97, the Library's Web-based catalogue (**opac97.bl.uk**), for consultation by those readers outside the Library. The British Library is currently introducing a new Web-based OPAC which will run alongside OPAC97 until the new system is thoroughly tested. An internal OPAC is available in the entrance hall and in the reading rooms at St Pancras for potential readers or visitors who are visiting the library in person for the first time. Although the Library is a general collection and not promoted specifically as a health library, there is a huge amount of health and medically-related material in the collections and the general nature of the collections allow access to subject areas which may be of interest to health care practitioners such as social services and community care. The periodicals held are listed on the website as well as printed in the *Current Serials in the British Library* publication which is issued annually. Hand lists of journals are also available for readers in the reading rooms.

Access to the collections is by reader's pass which can be obtained by filling in an application form which is available from the readers' admission office in the front hall at St Pancras. Passes range from one month to five years and will allow users access to all the collections held in the British Library at St Pancras for reference purposes only. The huge Document Supply Collections at Boston Spa may also be accessed from St Pancras with a 24 hour turnaround period. The Newspaper Library at Colindale operates on a similar system.

The Document Supply Centre at Boston Spa does possess a reading room but a phone call is required to ascertain whether there is room available (01937 546000). From this reading room one can access the vast collections of the British Library Document Supply Centre which provides a back up service for most of the libraries in the UK and many around the world. For borrowing purposes it is recommended that a user consults his or her local library first and requests an interlibrary loan (*see* Chapter 3).

The Health Care Information Service of the British Library (020 7412 7487) provides a quick enquiry service on health-related issues and the collections of the British Library available for consultation. There is also a service for more in-depth enquiries which is fee based and aimed at small to medium companies.

Independent libraries
The British Medical Association
BMA House, Tavistock Square, London WC1H 9JP. Tel: 020 7383 6625
(**http://www.bma.org.uk**)

The BMA Library is one of the three largest medical libraries in London (the British Library and the Royal Society of Medicine being the other two). It has a huge collection of clinical material but is a membership library primarily aimed at members of the Association. It is open to other health care professionals on a day ticket basis for a fee. Although the collection is primarily clinical material, the coverage is in great depth and there is an excellent audio-visual collection. The BMA Library also provides document supply and loans to both personal members and over 600 institutional members, the vast majority of which are NHS libraries. A good way therefore to access the BMA collection is via a local NHS library. The BMA also runs a successful Medline search service for BMA personal members.

The Royal Society of Medicine
1 Wimpole Street, London W1M 8AE. Tel: 020 7290 2940
(**http://www.rsm.org.uk**)

The RSM Library is the other major collection in London and covers a wider range of material than the BMA including many statistical works and research level material. It is also a membership library and has a day ticket system for a fee. If regular use of the collection is foreseen then becoming a fellow of the RSM may be worth considering.

in the US or through the network of the Medlars Centre around the world. NLM is a national resource for all US health science libraries through the National Network of Libraries of Medicine.

Research and development in the fields of librarianship and informatics is carried out by the Lister Hill National Center for Biomedical Communications (LHNCBC) and the National Center for Biotechnology Information (NCBI). The LHNCBC explores the uses of computer, communication, and audio-visual technologies to improve the organisation, dissemination, and utilisation of biomedical information. The Lister Hill Center has conducted a number of valuable experiments using NASA satellites, microwave and cable television, and computer-assisted instruction. Currently the Center is applying modern communications technologies to health care-related projects involving, for example, telemedicine, testbed networks and virtual reality.

The National Center for Biotechnology Information is developing information services for biotechnology – the task of storing and making accessible the staggering amounts of data about the human genome resulting from genetic research at the NIH and laboratories around the nation. NCBI also distributes GenBank, a collection of all known DNA sequences, and maintains the Human Gene Map on the World Wide Web at **http://www.ncbi.nlm.nih.gov/ genemap**.

The Toxicology and Environmental Health Program (TEHIP) established in 1967, is charged with setting up computer databases from the literature and from files of government and non-government organisations.

The NLM also organises tours of the building on Mondays through to Fridays.

GUIDE TO LIBRARIES AND INFORMATION SOURCES IN MEDICINE AND HEALTH CARE
Compiled by Peter Dale
With the assistance of Paul Wilson, 3rd EDITION

Whatever your subject interest, wherever you are, whoever you are this guide will provide useful and informative coverage of leading sources of information to help the work of librarians, information workers and researchers who need to know where specific information can be obtained. It covers those libraries and information services which are prepared to accept enquiries from outside, where a reasonable need exists.

- Check which organisations offer collections and services on your subject.
- Check contact details and Internet addresses.
- Check opening times and facilities.
- Check which organisations charge and which offer a basic free service.

An essential reference source
Besides medical, hospital and other health care libraries the guide includes details of a wide range of professional and voluntary organisations which are able to provide researchers with information. There is a wealth of material available from the many charities, support groups and voluntary bodies which can provide information for particular groups of people.

New edition
This 3rd edition takes account of the many former entries which have been merged/reorganised into NHS trusts. It also contains enhanced listings for Internet references.

Published by THE BRITISH LIBRARY November 2000
Price £40.00 (overseas postage extra)
215 pages, 297x210mm, paper, ISBN 0 7123 0856 3

Orders to Turpin Distribution Services Ltd, Blackhorse Road, Letchworth, Herts SG6 1HN, UK. Tel 01462 672555, Fax 01462 480497, Email turpin@turpinltd.com